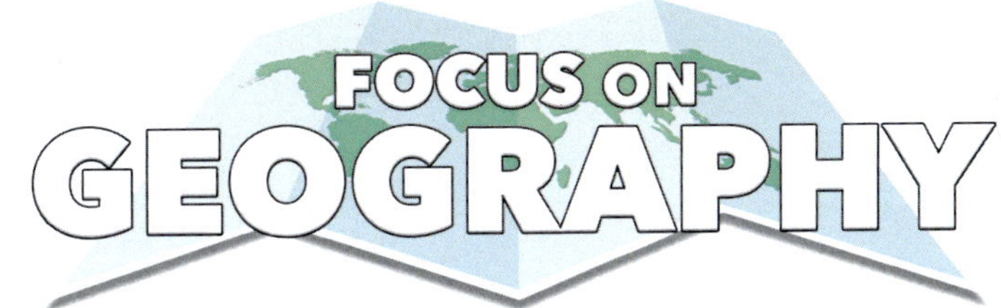

Focus on Mexico

Linda Barghoorn

Crabtree Publishing

crabtreebooks.com

Crabtree Publishing

crabtreebooks.com 800-387-7650

In Canada: We acknowledge the financial support of the Government of Canada through the Canada Book Fund for our publishing activities.

Author: Linda Barghoorn
Series research and development: Janine Deschenes
Editorial director: Kathy Middleton
Editor: Janine Deschenes
Proofreader: Roseann Biederman
Design: Tammy McGarr
Print and production coordinator: Tammy McGarr

Hardcover	978-1-0396-6316-9
Paperback	978-1-0396-6375-6
Ebook (pdf)	978-1-0396-6818-8
Epub	978-1-0396-8558-1
Read-along	978-1-0396-8607-6
Audio book	978-1-0396-6867-6

Printed in Canada/012024/CPC20240117

Library and Archives Canada Cataloguing in Publication
Available at the Library and Archives Canada

Library of Congress Cataloging-in-Publication Data
Available at the Library of Congress

Published in Canada
Crabtree Publishing
616 Welland Avenue
St. Catharines, Ontario
L2M 5V6

Published in the United States Crabtree Publishing
347 Fifth Avenue
Suite 1402-145
New York, NY 10016

IMAGE CREDITS
Alamy
REUTERS - Alamy Stock Photo: p. 31 (bottom)
Creative Commons
Thelmadatter: p. 5, Alejandro Vega Rdz.: p. 11 (bo om), p. 15 (top right)
iStock
FG Trade: Front cover (top left), Photo Beto: p. 4 op), p. 37 (bottom), p. 42 (bottom), ferrantraite: p. 14, ZU_09: p. 22 (bottom), holgs: p. 34
Public Domain
public domain United States José Díaz del Castillo: p. 23 (bottom)
Shutterstock
Kobby Dagan: title page, FERNANDO MACIAS ROMO: p. 7 (bottom right), ChameleonsEye: p. 19 op), p. 32, SHCHERBAKOV SERHII: p. 22 op), Kertu: p. 24 (top), Jon Nicholls Photography: p. 27, Adam Melnyk: p. 28 (top), Ungureanu Catalina Oana: p. 29 (bottom), carlos.araujo: p. 33 (top), ezellhphotography: p. 33 (bo om), Marcelo Rodriguez: p. 36 (top), Bisual Photo: p. 36 (bottom and bottom left), Carolina Arroyo: p. 38 (top right), Roberto Galan: p. 39 op and bottom), clicksdemexico: p. 40 (top), Octavio Hoyos: p. 40 (bottom), Eduardo_ Chavez: p. 41, Sergey-73: p. 44 (bottom left), eddie-hernandez.com: p. 45 (bottom)
All other images from Shutterstock

Contents

INTRODUCTION

Life in Hidalgo

The Otomí are an **Indigenous** people who live in the Mexican Highlands of the Sierra Madres mountains. There, the mountain slopes give way to a **fertile plateau** with relatively cool temperatures and moderate rainfall—an ideal place for growing crops for food.

The Otomí are the original settlers of the area. They created the powerful, ancient city of Teotihuacan. Most live as their ancestors did for centuries—as subsistence farmers, known as *campesinos*. Subsistence farmers grow just what they need to support themselves and their families. Their adobe houses are scattered across the hilltops. These mud-brick dwellings are constructed of local materials. Their thick walls create a cool interior, protected from the heat of the midday Sun.

Often, adobe houses have just an earth floor and simple furniture: beds, a table and chairs, and a small cooking area.

The Sierra Madres mountains have western, eastern, and southern ranges.

Rich Traditions

Typical crops grown by the Otomí are corn, beans, squash, and chiles. Most people own small plots of land for farming. Corn was **domesticated** there around 9,000 years ago from a local grass. It looks very little like the corn we know today. It has been a staple in Mexican food ever since. Most mornings begin with a simple breakfast of corn tortillas and black beans. Mothers grind the corn on a metate, or a stone mortar and pestle. Then, they mix it with water, form the mixture into tortillas, and cook the tortillas on a large pan over an open fire.

Family is a key ingredient in Mexican life. Often three generations—grandparents, parents, and children—live together in one house. Everyone shares in daily chores, from tending the crops to cooking, cleaning, and fetching water. A hammock strung between trees might offer a quiet place for an afternoon *siesta*, or nap. This was once a common practice throughout the country. Weekend markets give families the chance to travel to town. They can purchase needed goods and meet up with friends.

The Otomí are known for creating tenango embroidery, seen here. This beautiful art is bright, colorful, and often depicts the plants, animals, and everyday life of Mexico.

Mexico is the southernmost country in North America and shares a long border with the United States. It has two long coastlines, with the Pacific Ocean on its west coast and the Gulf of Mexico to its east. Its southern border is the gateway to the Central American countries of Guatemala and Belize. The country also has a diverse range of landscapes—from **barren** deserts to tropical rain forests, **craggy** mountain peaks, coastal mangrove swamps, and fertile plateaus and valleys. The Tropic of Cancer divides Mexico into **temperate** northern zones and **subtropical** zones to the south.

AT A GLANCE

- **OFFICIAL NAME:** United Mexican States
- **NATIONAL CAPITAL:** Mexico City
- **POPULATION:** 127,276,000
- **OFFICIAL LANGUAGE:** Spanish
- **LAND AREA:** 756,470 square miles (1,959,248 sq. km)

Mangrove swamps are found in tropical and subtropical areas. They have brackish, or slightly salty, water. The mangroves in Mexico are home to unique plant and animal species, such as the crocodile (left).

The ruins of the ancient Aztec city of Tenochtitlán are found in modern-day Mexico City. The Spanish arrived there in 1519. For years, they battled with the Aztecs for control. After Tenochtitlán fell to the Spanish, they built their own city atop its ruins.

The People of Mexico

Mexico was first inhabited by Indigenous peoples who migrated there thousands of years ago. They were traditionally hunters and farmers. Their incredible legacy includes two of the world's most magnificent ancient civilizations: the Aztecs and the Mayans. Today's *Indígenas* are the descendants of these people. More than 60 Indigenous peoples live in Mexico today and represent approximately 20 percent of its population.

Spanish **conquistadors** arrived in the 1500s, in search of new land to **colonize** and following rumors of Mexico's rich mineral resources. Today, most Mexicans are mestizos—of mixed Indigenous and Spanish heritage. Most practice the Roman Catholic religion brought from Spain. However, traditional Indigenous beliefs—which hold a strong connection to nature and the environment—still play an important role in everyday life and culture throughout the country.

Many of Mexico's large cities—and, indeed, much of the country's population today—are located on the Mesa Central, a large plateau of fertile land. It is known as "Mexico's breadbasket" because it is the source of food crops that support much of the country.

Crops grown in the Mesa Central, such as sugar, coffee, and fruits and vegetables, are also exported abroad. Much of Mexico's exports go to the United States.

CHAPTER 1

The Land

Tucked Between Mountains

The Sierra Madres mountain ranges dominate much of Mexico's land. They isolate areas from one another, making human migration and settlement challenging. Tucked between these ranges, however, are two regions that contain the most fertile land in the country: the Mesa Central and the Volcanic Axis. Their rich soils, temperate climates, and annual rainfalls created the perfect conditions for agriculture and human settlement. Today, they are the most densely populated regions of the country. Many of Mexico's largest cities, including Guadalajara, León, and Puebla, are found there.

Coastal Areas

As the Sierra Madres descend towards Mexico's coastlines, they create striking and varied landscapes. In some places, the rough mountainous coasts offer little opportunity for settlement. Other coastlands consist of swampy lagoons and mangrove wetlands. Much of Mexico's southern coastal areas are vulnerable to tropical cyclones, monsoons, and hurricanes. These can cause significant damage to coastal cities and towns. Along the southern Gulf Coast, a dramatic coastline known as the Mexican Riviera is popular with tourists looking for subtropical temperatures and long sunny days.

Puebla, located in the Volcanic Axis near Mexico City, is home to more than 3.2 million people. It began as a Spanish colonial city and was an important point on the route between Mexico City and the port of Veracruz on the Gulf of Mexico.

Southern Highlands

A series of disconnected mountain ranges and plateaus, including the southern Sierra Madres mountains, form the Southern Highlands. They have served as effective barriers to human settlement, isolating this region from the rest of the country. Today it is one of the least developed, most sparsely populated, and poorest in Mexico. It is home to a number of Indigenous tribes. But it is difficult terrain for the subsistence farmers who live there.

Unnavigable Rivers

Because of Mexico's largely mountainous terrain, many of its rivers are fast-flowing and dangerous to navigate. The Rio Grande—Mexico's largest—forms much of the northern Mexican border with the United States. Some rivers have been dammed to irrigate fields for crops. The Rio Grande, in fact, provides water to more than 2.1 million acres (850,000 hectares) of cropland in Mexico and the U.S. The Balsas River, in south-central Mexico, is a significant source for hydroelectric power.

Wildlife and Agriculture

Mexico's wildlife and plant species are as varied as its landscapes. In the harsh Sonoran Desert in Mexico's northeast, a variety of cacti thrive. Indigenous peoples harvested prickly pear fruit for food. They also used juice from the fruit to dye textiles and even used its prickly spikes as needles. Yucca plants also were useful in making goods such as clothing, footwear, rope, and baskets. The Aztecs harvested the agave plant to create a fermented drink called pulque. It is the precursor to one of Mexico's most popular exports today: tequila. Pulque is still produced and enjoyed locally in Mexico.

A number of marine species live off Mexico's coasts. The largest is the gray whale, which breeds in the warm Pacific Ocean waters. The Gulf of Mexico and Pacific Ocean teem with fish and shellfish—from snapper, tuna, and anchovies to lobster and shrimp. Coastal cities have developed around Mexico's fishing industry. Mountainous regions are home to puma, coyote, and deer, some of which are featured in traditional Indigenous dances and ceremonies. Tropical rain forests provide lush habitats for monkeys, parrots, quetzal birds, jaguars, and tapirs. Indigenous peoples used trees for woodcarving, medicines, dyes, and **resin**.

The unique shape of the cirio, or boojum tree, stands out amidst the **sparse** scrub vegetation of the Sonoran Desert. It reaches up to 50 feet (15 m) tall.

Forests cover approximately one-third of Mexico's land area. The plant and animal species there make Mexico one of the most biodiverse countries in the world. However, **deforestation** and the effects of climate change, such as more droughts and forest fires, put Mexico's forests at risk.

Closer Look

Mexican Plateau

The fertile soils of the Mexican Plateau, a high, flat area between two Sierra Madre mountain ranges, attracted **nomadic** hunters who settled there more than 11,000 years ago. They began collecting the wild plants that grew there, before developing methods to farm crops. They were the first to domesticate wild grass into the corn that is such a staple in the Mexican diet. Other staples were beans and squash. The higher altitudes of the plateau provided a temperate climate with abundant rainfall—more suitable for crops than the climate in coastal regions. Small settlements there prospered and grew into magnificent empires, such as the Aztec Empire. When the Spaniards arrived, they expanded agriculture further to include wheat, sugar cane, citrus fruits, and rice.

The Mexican Plateau is made up of the Mesa Del Norte in the north and the Mesa Central in the south. The latter region is smaller, but much more populated.

Natural Resources

Mexico is rich in natural resources and has strong fishing and agricultural industries. **Commercial** crops, such as coffee, avocado, and tomatoes, are grown in areas with irrigated farmland. Large shrimping grounds are found in the Gulf of California. Most commercial fishing is done there, with other catches including lobster, tuna, sardines, and anchovies. The Sierra Madre mountains hold precious deposits of silver, gold, copper, lead, and zinc. Much of the country's mining activity is found in the northwest states of Durango, Chihuahua, and Zacatecas. Sonora state has the country's largest gold mine.

Timber

While some forests are logged for valuable timber, such as oak, mahogany, and rosewood, many have been cleared to make way for expanding human settlement and livestock farming. The introduction of livestock by the Spanish more than 400 years ago created an enormous demand for animal grazing land. Large swaths of forest were destroyed, changing the landscape dramatically and damaging wildlife habitats. Another threat to Mexico's forests is climate change. Warmer temperatures mean that the forests are more vulnerable to fires and insect infestations. It's estimated that Mexico has lost more than half of its original forests.

Mineral wealth enticed Spanish explorers who exploited these resources and sent much of the wealth back to Spain. Colonial cities sprang up around mining sites. Taxco (pictured) is one example, where silver is still mined and made into products.

Illegal logging is a problem across Mexico. It is often carried out by crime groups, which often force locals to work as loggers. The groups then sell the wood to build homes and furniture all over Mexico. The lack of regulation of this logging worsens deforestation.

Oil

Significant oil **reserves** have been found in Mexico. In 2020, the country produced 1.9 million barrels of oil per day. The oil industry is an important part of Mexico's economy. Commercial oil production in the country was underway by 1901. Its development was pushed forward by the building of Mexico's national railway system.

Campeche, in the southern Yucatan state, took its name from the Spanish pronunciation of the Mayan Ah Kin Pech, meaning "the place of serpents and ticks." This rather unpleasant environment was one of the first landing sites of the Spanish conquistadors. In the 1970s, oil was discovered in the shallow waters of Campeche Bay, which expanded Mexico's oil production. Today offshore wells supply Mexico with oil and natural gas for its modern economy. More than 100,000 people work for Mexico's national oil company, Petróleos Mexicanos (Pemex).

The United Nations Educational, Scientific, and Cultural Organization (UNESCO) recognize the town of Campeche as a **World Heritage Site**. This is because of its well-preserved colonial architecture.

Prosperity and Poverty

Today, more than half of Mexico's people live in the Mexican Plateau region, where the climate is more pleasant than the tropical coastal areas. The region is the heart of Mexico's economy. Much of the country's manufacturing, **commerce**, and industries are located there. The modern, urban lifestyle of its big cities—Mexico City, Guadalajara, Puebla, and Leon, to name a few—seems worlds away from the traditional way of life in more isolated, rural areas.

Four out of five Mexicans live in an urban area. Many of these areas have experienced huge shifts in culture and lifestyle as they modernize to compete in the global economy. *Mestizos*, or people of mixed Indigenous and Spanish heritage, make up the majority of the population. They control much of the country's economic and political power through roles that have been handed down within families for many generations.

BAJA CALIFORNIA

SONORA

BAJA CALIFORNIA SUR

About two-thirds of Mexican workers are employed in the service sector, in jobs in industries such as tourism, transportation, food, and education.

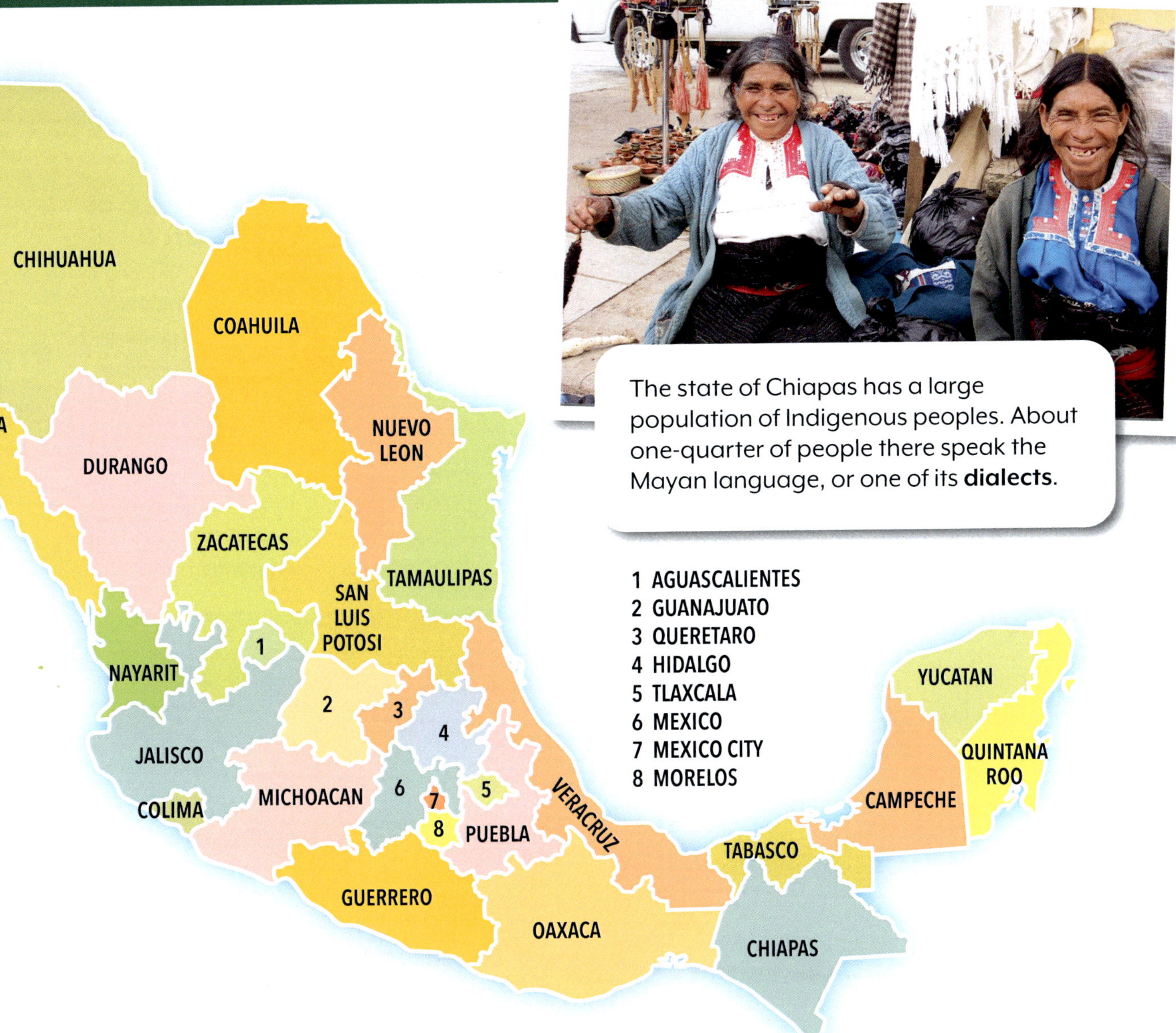

The state of Chiapas has a large population of Indigenous peoples. About one-quarter of people there speak the Mayan language, or one of its **dialects**.

Rural Life

Vast areas of Mexico's more barren northern terrain and its tropical southern areas are much more sparsely populated and much poorer. Many of Mexico's Indígenas continue to inhabit these regions. Much of the Indigenous population has been **marginalized** since the days the Spanish invaded and colonized Mexico. Those who speak Indigenous languages rather than Spanish—the working language of the country—have had fewer opportunities for education, jobs, and future success.

The poorest three states in Mexico—Chiapas, Guerrero, and Oaxaca—are in the southernmost part of the country. There, Indígena farmers live in small **communal** villages. Many follow traditions and lifestyles that have lasted for centuries. Many of their communities are remote, separated by mountains and difficult terrain. This has made economic development much more challenging. Increasingly, people from poor areas like these are migrating to Mexico's cities in search of work, education, and a better life.

CHAPTER 2

Becoming Mexico

Ancient Peoples

As nomadic hunters settled on the Mexican Plateau, they found a range of wild plants that they cultivated into regular, seasonal crops. Corn was domesticated from a wild grass, followed by avocados, chili peppers, beans, squashes, and amaranth (an ancient grain). By 2000 B.C.E., whole villages had grown up around and were sustained by agriculture. These single, isolated villages were the building blocks for the more complex societies that followed.

Olmec Peoples

Mexico's first known society is believed to be the Olmecs, who settled on the Gulf of Mexico around 3,000 years ago. They established a trade center at San Lorenzo in the modern-day province of Veracruz. Its strategic inland position protected it from coastal flooding. At the same time, its location near the coast allowed the Olmecs to control regional trade. Olmec religion was strongly tied to nature. Special significance was placed in the belief that the heavens, earth, and underworld, or world of the dead, are connected.

The Olmecs are known for the giant statues of human heads that were discovered beginning in 1862. A total of 17 have been discovered, from four sites where the Olmec settled. It is thought that they represented powerful rulers, as each has a unique headdress.

Today, tourists can visit the ancient ruins of Teotihuacan, just east of modern day Mexico City. Two main pyramids can be seen there: The Pyramid of the Moon, and the Pyramid of the Sun (below), one of the biggest pyramids in the world.

Teotihuacan

By 300 B.C.E., agricultural villages had sprung up across southern Mexico. The powerful city of Teotihuacan was established in the Valley of Mexico around 100 B.C.E. A collection of Maya, Mixtec, and Zapotec Indigenous peoples lived there. One theory is that different villagers fled there after a volcanic eruption. Teotihuacan quickly became the most powerful and influential city in the region. Its wealth came from the trade of locally made goods and resources. These included tools made of **obsidian**, ceramics, cotton, and exotic bird feathers. It is estimated that at its peak, 150,000 to 200,000 people lived in the city. At the time, it was one of the largest in the world. Little is known about what happened to this civilization, however. It is possible that rival invaders from the north overthrew the city.

Ongoing **excavations** to learn more about the lost civilization have led to the discoveries of an ancient tunnel system, human and animal remains, paintings, and artifacts such as stone tools.

Chichén Itzá is an ancient Mayan city and the site of ruins such as this well-known pyramid. The combined number of steps on the pyramid is 365—the number of days it takes for Earth to make one rotation around the Sun.

The Mayans

Several centuries after the decline of Teotihuacan, the Mayans created one of the most spectacular ancient civilizations humankind has ever known. Unlike many others who preferred drier, more temperate climates, the Mayans thrived in their tropical, rainforest setting. The mountainous terrain and few navigable rivers provided both protection from invasion and relative isolation. They relied heavily on local resources. Buildings were made of local limestone. Jade and exotic feathers decorated the elaborate costumes of the nobles. Shells were used as trumpets during warfare and religious ceremonies. Religion was part of everyday life for the Mayans. They worshipped gods related to elements of the natural world: the Sun, Moon, rain, and—of course—corn! They studied the position of stars and planets in an effort to determine when best to plant their crops. After more than 600 years, the civilization collapsed around 900 C.E. The cause of the collapse is a mystery. Theories include overpopulation, environmental damage, or a long drought.

This ancient Mayan observatory in the city of Chichén Itzá was one of the locations where the Mayans observed changes in the sky and space objects.

The Aztecs

Legend claims that an Aztec god, Huitzilopochtli, commanded his nomadic people to search for a permanent home. According to legend, it would be revealed by an eagle resting on a cactus with a serpent in its beak. Their thirteenth century capital city, Tenochtitlán, was constructed on a small island in Lake Texcoco where the Aztecs found this eagle. The Aztecs' power was based on their incredible agricultural accomplishments. They developed sophisticated **irrigation** systems and a system of floating gardens in shallow lakes known as *chiampas*. The mild climate and plentiful water supplies provided multiple harvests each year. The population grew rapidly as food became plentiful. The valley's system of lakes and artificial canals enabled extensive transportation and trade. This allowed the Aztecs to hold considerable economic and political control over the region.

People celebrate Aztec history and folklore in Mexico City, where the ancient city of Tenochtitlán was located.

The Nahuas, descendants of the Aztecs, are the largest Indigenous group in Mexico. More than 1.5 million people speak some variation of Náhuatl, the language of the Aztecs.

Spanish Invasion

In the 1500s, Spanish conquistadors set out from Spain in search of new lands to enrich their country's wealth. They landed on the Yucatan Peninsula in 1517 and established a base. From there, they set out into Mexico's interior. They arrived at the Aztec city of Tenochtitlán in 1519, which they captured and then destroyed. By 1521 they had established a new capital there. It was the foundation of modern-day Mexico City. **Missionaries** from Spain's Catholic Church arrived, intending to spread their religion to Indigenous peoples. Spanish colonizers spent the following decades expanding their influence across Mexico. They created new cities and towns around the natural resources they exploited.

Colonization of northern Mexico was more challenging because of the climate and the terrain. But the Spanish persisted. They were motivated by dreams of precious minerals and the need to establish defenses against other invaders. They built colonial mining towns and **exploited** mineral deposits that had been unearthed by Indigenous peoples centuries earlier. Many of these resources were shipped back to Spain.

indigo plant

The Spanish also developed an appetite for items Indigenous peoples had developed from local plants. **Cochineal** and **indigo** dyes were prized by Europe's growing **textile** industry. Cacao crops were expanded to meet Europe's demand for the treat known today as chocolate. Vanilla, sugar, cotton, and tobacco were also harvested for overseas markets.

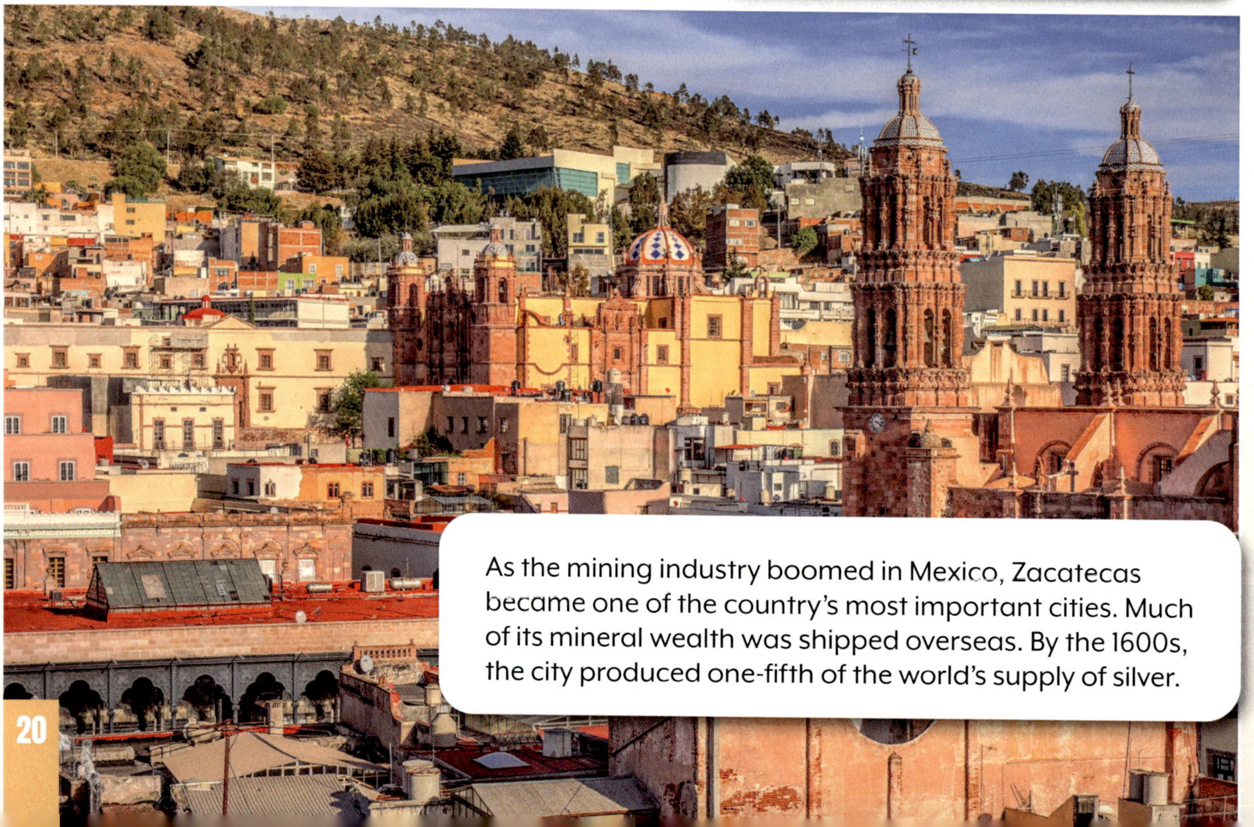

As the mining industry boomed in Mexico, Zacatecas became one of the country's most important cities. Much of its mineral wealth was shipped overseas. By the 1600s, the city produced one-fifth of the world's supply of silver.

Closer Look

Success at the Expense of Indigenous Peoples

After destroying Tenochtitlán and overtaking the Aztec empire, the Spanish enslaved many of its Indigenous inhabitants. Agriculture and mining takes a lot of labor. The Spanish did not have thousands of strong workers to do this labor, so they relied on the slave labor of Indigenous peoples. Their economic success in this new colony was due to this forced labor, as well as the forced labor of enslaved Africans who were brought to the colony across the Atlantic Ocean.

The Spanish also brought thousands of enslaved people from Africa to its new colony in Mexico. Some mestizos today are their descendants.

Millions of Indigenous peoples also died of diseases brought by the Spanish. They were susceptible to these new diseases, as they did not have natural immunity. A smallpox outbreak in Tenochtitlán was a major contributor to its downfall to the Spanish. The disease spread through the densely populated city, killing an estimated half of its population, including its ruler. There were also **epidemics** of smallpox, measles, **cocoliztli**, and others. These diseases, coupled with war, famine, and the brutal treatment of enslaved people decimated the Indigenous population in Mexico. Some estimates say that 80 to 90 percent were killed.

The Maya were also heavily impacted by European diseases. Some researchers think disease could have been a reason for the civilization's mysterious downfall.

Building the New World

Less than 50 years after their arrival, Spanish conquerors controlled much of the Aztec empire. Race and wealth determined a person's status in Mexico's colonial society. "Whites," or European-born settlers, and mestizos, or mixed white and Indigenous people, took control of the land and positions of authority. The most powerful people were Spaniards who were sent from Spain to rule the colony, and their descendants.

Indigenous people in many of Spain's colonies resisted the encomienda system. One example is the Taino rebellion in modern day Dominican Republic, led by the *cacique*, or chief, Enriquillo (above). The system was abolished by 1791.

Many Indigenous owners were pushed off their land. They were enslaved or forced to work for wealthy Spanish landowners. The Spanish implemented the encomienda system in its colonies. Under this system, Indigenous people were forced to give free labor and tribute, or payment, to Spanish landowners in return for protection. In practice, it was a form of enslavement under which people were worked to death. Small Indigenous-owned farms were replaced by large, livestock ranches that supplied the settlers' growing demand for meat. Huge areas of forest were cleared, destroying animal habitats and altering the landscape forever.

New seaports, such as Veracruz, were built on the Gulf of Mexico as trade with Spain and the Americas grew.

This statue of Miguel Hidalgo y Costilla stands in the city of Dolores Hidalgo, where the Mexican War of Independence began with his call to action.

Industrialization and the Rise of Cities

As agriculture and mining industries grew, cities expanded. They became trade hubs and industrial centers, where goods were processed. Mining cities such as Zacatecas, San Luis Potosi, and Guanajuato were vital to Mexico's economy as Spain's demand for silver multiplied. Other cities, like Puebla, Leon, and Guadalajara prospered as production centers for the country's agricultural goods.

A series of uprisings took place in the 1800s as Mexico's poor and working-class people demanded better rights and access to land. But little changed for them. By the end of the century, the government made changes to modernize the country. Roads and railways were expanded. Maquiladores—foreign-owned industries—were built to advance the country's economic growth. Cities grew more prosperous, but much of this growth benefitted only the country's wealthy and most powerful families.

Between 1810 and 1821, revolts occurred across Mexico in response to Spain's injustices toward the country's poor. Led by Miguel Hidalgo y Costilla, together the revolts are known as the Mexican War of Independence. It ended Spanish rule of the country.

CHAPTER 3 Life Today

Most people in Mexico speak Spanish, which is the language used in schools. There are also more than 50 Indigenous languages used in the country. Students in both public and private schools in Mexico wear uniforms.

Many households in Mexico have several generations of a family living together. Family life is important and members of an extended family often maintain close ties.

Living in Modern Mexico

Life throughout much of Mexico has changed from a largely rural and agricultural society to a modern, urbanized one. Most Mexicans are either mestizo or Indígena. Membership in one of these two groups plays an enormous role in where and how a person lives in Mexico.

Mestizos make up the largest portion of the Mexican population: approximately two-thirds. They have controlled much of Mexico's industry and wealth since the country was colonized. Land ownership—seized from Indigenous owners—was passed along from one generation to the next. This ensured that much of the country's resources and wealth remained in the hands of a few wealthy families. Most of Mexico's mestizos live in urban settings where there is better access to housing, education, health care, and jobs. These services provide opportunities that are unavailable to Mexico's more rural population.

Closer Look

Life for Indígenas

While Mexicans are immensely proud of their ancient Indigenous cultures, the treatment of Indigenous peoples has often been unjust. Many Indígenas were exploited by Spanish colonizers and continue to be discriminated against today. Indigenous families often live in the least developed, poorest regions of Mexico. Those who don't own land must rely on poorly paid day-labor jobs to support their families. Often, Indigenous communities lack basic necessities, such as safe housing, and services such as health care and education. Without access to these services and well-paid jobs, many are unable to improve their chances for a better future. Despite repeated uprisings and protests from Indigenous communities, the government has done little to help them improve their economic status.

Housing in Indigenous communities is often crowded and without running water and electricity. However, efforts are being made to build safe and sustainable housing in states such as Puebla and Chiapas.

Cultural traditions are central to daily life. They include games, celebrations, and art, such as this colorful embroidery.

Many Indígenas still practice subsistence farming. However, large-scale agricultural activities, such as logging, mining, and ranching, are threats to their land and way of life.

The Wealthy Neighbor Next Door

Mexico's border with the United States—an economic powerhouse—has had an enormous impact on Mexico's economy and culture. It has grown into the world's ninth largest economy by developing its natural resources, growing its manufacturing base, and expanding its exports. These activities are often supported by American policies and financing.

NAFTA

The North American Free Trade Agreement (NAFTA) was established in 1994 between Mexico, Canada, and the United States. It was designed to improve opportunities for business and trade between the three countries. In doing so, it created the largest **free market** in the world. This opened up new opportunities for economic growth. NAFTA provided the United States with a new way to export American-made goods to Mexican consumers. Mexicans were therefore introduced to food and products that were not previously part of their culture or lifestyle. Mexico's exports also increased dramatically with NAFTA. Nearly 90 percent went to the U.S.

NAFTA brought many new jobs to Mexico. American companies opened factories there, where wages were much lower than in the United States. This meant that products for foreign markets, such as electronics and cars, could be produced more cheaply.

Maquiladores

Before NAFTA, the program to build foreign-owned maquiladores helped redistribute some of Mexico's wealth and population away from Mexico City. A maquiladora is a manufacturing operation by a foreign-owned company that makes goods for export. Many maquiladores were located in towns like Tijuana and Juarez, near the U.S. border. This supported cross-border trade. However, as transportation routes improved, the locations of maquiladores expanded to other regions across the country. They have played important roles in building the country's automobile, aerospace, chemical, and textile industries.

Human Migration

Extreme poverty has forced many of Mexico's rural poor to seek opportunities elsewhere. Many have become seasonal migrant workers in both the United States and Canada. They often do so through government programs that help workers meet the labor needs of farmers in each country. Workers spend months away from home each year, harvesting agricultural crops and sending their earnings back to their families in Mexico. The lifestyle and culture they are introduced to often sharply contrast with their traditional values and beliefs. Many countries depend on seasonal migrant workers. However, they are sometimes vulnerable to poor working and living conditions and can be exploited on the farms where they work. The risk of being **deported** often keeps these workers from speaking out against mistreatment.

The COVID-19 pandemic, which began in 2020, made living and working conditions more **precarious** for seasonal migrant workers. They were more vulnerable to catching and spreading the virus in shared, often-poor living arrangements. It was also often impossible to social distance at work.

Regional Industries

Mexico has a broad base of natural resources, which it has used to build its modern economy. Some of the major industries related to natural resources include agriculture, tourism, fishing, mining, shipping, and oil. The service industry is also a main part of Mexico's economy, which includes trade, transportation, finance, and government jobs.

Agriculture

Much of Mexico's wealth and population is based in the Valley of Mexico, the heartland of its rich agricultural traditions. Cities like Guadalajara and Leon have grown up around regional crops of corn, livestock, sugar cane, and wheat. Large-scale farms whose products are exported across North America have replaced subsistence farming.

Tourism

The rugged coastlines of the Southern Highlands are known as the Mexican Riviera. Direct flights from the United States and Canada have made this a key destination for tourists escaping northern winters. They come to enjoy Mexico's food, cultural diversity, and tropical climate. Many resorts are located in Mexico's poorest regions, but the locals who work there rarely benefit from the tourism economy.

Some people sell goods such as jewelry and clothing to tourists near large resorts. **Informal jobs** such as these are essential in Mexico where the minimum wage is low.

Almost one-fifth of workers in Mexico are employed in the agriculture industry.

Mexico produces more than 6 million pounds (2.7 million kilograms) of silver each year.

Fishing

Fisheries are located on the coasts of the Pacific Ocean and the Gulf of Mexico. Catches include lobster, shrimp, tuna, and anchovies. Processing plants in coastal cities like Veracruz prepare catches for export overseas.

Mining

Spanish colonizers were responsible for establishing the roots of Mexico's mining industry. The cities they built near silver deposits are known today as the Silver Belt. It stretches across the Mexican Plateau. Mexico is the world's largest producer of silver. Zinc is another important mineral export.

Shipping

Veracruz, on the Gulf of Mexico, was the main coastal link between Mexico and Spain during colonial times. Today it is an important international seaport. It handles large volumes of products exported from Mexico around the world.

Oil

Mexico's state-owned oil company is a major source of income for the government. However, it has also been the target of environmentalists and land-rights activists. In some coastal regions, Indigenous communities were forced off their lands to make way for developments to support the offshore oil industry.

The Pacific Ocean port of Manzanillo, in the province of Colima, is Mexico's largest in terms of the amount of cargo going in and out.

Human Impact on the Environment

Human settlement and **industrialization** have dramatically changed Mexico's landscapes and environment. Large areas of rain forest were destroyed to make way for growing cities and large farms. While the government claims it has enacted measures to reduce deforestation and protect the environment, environmentalists suggest that the destruction has continued at unacceptable levels.

The introduction of livestock by Spanish settlers displaced many wildlife species because huge areas of land were cleared for grazing. Mining and logging operations have also **encroached** on wildlife habitats. Air pollution and logging activities have threatened the habitats of monarch butterflies, for example. Their spectacular annual migration between Mexico and the United States and Canada has been devastated due to habitat loss.

The monarch population has declined dramatically. Experts say the species could become extinct in the next few decades if nothing is done to save them.

Communities in Mexico are fighting deforestation. Communities in the Lacandon rain forest in the south of Mexico, for example, have taken up **eco-tourism** to promote forest conservation. They are hoping for more support from the Mexican government.

The Unintended Consequences of NAFTA

To compete with the enormous agricultural industry of the United States, many of Mexico's small farms have been replaced with large, industrial-scale ones. Often, they focus on a single crop, known as a monoculture. This is a radical change from the age-old method of **interplanting** crops, which naturally support one another against pests and drought. The use of pesticides and fertilizers has become common as a result. As Mexico's economy moved from an agricultural to an industrial one, it has also experienced an increase in air and water pollution in many urban areas.

Mining emissions and fertilizers and pesticides used for farming have contaminated many local water supplies.

Environmental Laws

In 1988, Mexico enacted a series of environmental laws to deal with its growing economy and environmental challenges. The NAFTA agreement includes regulations to address environmental issues. However, they are not always well enforced. The Border 2025 Program between the United States and Mexico is designed to work toward **sustainable** development while addressing mutual environmental issues. Mexico has also committed to goals outlined in the 2015 Paris Climate Agreement.

The Paris Climate Agreement is an international agreement about climate change. Its goal is to limit global warming by reducing emissions and moving toward low- or zero-**carbon** solutions.

CHAPTER 4

A Vibrant Country

What Makes Mexico Special?

Mexico's unique and complex identity comes from the combination of the country's ancient cultures and beliefs and the new way of life of the Spanish colonizers. The impact of the economy and culture of the United States has also been significant in shaping modern Mexico. Mexico's languages, foods, traditions, and beliefs are as diverse as its many distinct landscapes. Most urban Mexicans embrace a blend of modern attitudes, traditional values, and occasionally even ancient superstitions. *Curanderos*, or traditional Indigenous healers or medicine men, for example, are still popular with some people who prefer them over modern doctors.

The Spanish missionaries who arrived in the 1500s and 1600s converted Indigenous peoples to the Catholic religion only by inserting it alongside traditional beliefs and rituals. Old gods took on new names as Christian saints. Indigenous festivals were blended with Christian feasts and celebrations. While most Mexicans have adopted Christianity as their religion, powerful Aztec gods like the goddess of the Earth, Nakawe, continue to play important roles in daily life.

The Metropolitan Cathedral in Mexico City is the oldest and largest cathedral in **Latin America** and an important religious center. It is not uncommon to see *concheros*, or Aztec dancers, outside it performing a dance that bridges Catholic and Indigenous traditions.

Strong Community Ties

Mexicans take great pride in their reputation as warm and hospitable people. A strong sense of family and community are central to life in Mexico. Time with friends and family is an essential part of daily life. From the early days of settlement, town squares played an important role as gathering places on evenings and weekends. There, families and friends eat, celebrate, dance, and share news of one another's lives. This is still the case today even in Mexico's bustling, modern cities. Leisure time is important, and the many colorful festivals celebrated throughout the year play a lively role of the rhythm of Mexican life.

Soccer, or football as it is known in Mexico, is the country's most popular sport.

It is common for large, extended Mexican families to gather for celebrations such as the *quinceañera*, or girl's 15th birthday party.

Daily Life

Mexico City is the beating heart of modern Mexico and one of the most densely populated cities in the world. About one in every six Mexicans live there. While Mexico's rural regions have maintained many of the traditional ways of life, Mexico City is more modern in its attitudes, lifestyle, and values.

As modern influences spread throughout Mexico's cities, some traditions have begun to change. Midday meals were traditionally large meals where entire families gathered to share food, gossip, and stories. Often an afternoon siesta, or nap, would follow before children returned to school, and men and women returned to work. In many urban areas today, however, longer commutes make it impossible to return home for a leisurely lunch. More demanding work schedules also mean longer hours and fewer siestas.

In smaller villages and tourist areas, open-air markets are still common. There, everything from locally grown fruits and vegetables to clothing is sold. Many traditional *abarrotes*—small grocery stores selling local goods—have been replaced by modern supermarkets with larger selections and imported items.

A variety of fruits and vegetables are for sale in this open-air market in San Cristobal, in southern Mexico.

A *sarape* is a traditional blanket-like shawl worn as a coat. It is usually brightly colored and has a fringe. It is especially worn by men.

sombrero

Clothing and Family Traditions

While many urban Mexicans have traded traditional clothing for more modern looks, many people in rural communities continue to enjoy the traditional styles. These might include hats with wide brims for protection from the Sun, such as *sombreros*, and clothing made of locally grown cotton. Many women's costumes feature colorful ribbons and embroidery. Loose-fitting blouses and long skirts are popular choices.

Family remains at the center of all Mexican traditions and values. Many households—whether in modern cities or remote rural areas—continue to consist of multiple generations living together. All family members are expected to take part in household chores and caring for the children.

Huipiles are a traditional garment worn by some of Mexico's Indigenous women.

Dia de la Independencia, on September 16, is a day celebrated by the entire country of Mexico. It commemorates the start of Mexico's War of Independence.

Festivals and Celebrations

Life in Mexico can be colorful and lively. *Fiestas*, or festivals, are a big part of this vibrancy. There are many reasons to celebrate in Mexico. Some fiestas have evolved from ancient Aztec celebrations. Others were inspired by Spanish culture and beliefs.

On October 12, Mexicans observe *Dia de la Raza*, or "Race Day." It celebrates the multicultural nature of modern Mexico and acknowledges the Indigenous peoples who were harmed by the Spanish colonization of Mexico.

Guelaguetza is celebrated every July in Oaxaca region. In Aztec times, human sacrifices were made as an offering to the Aztec god of maize, Centeotl, to provide a plentiful harvest. When the Spanish arrived, they replaced these sacrifices with Christian elements. Today's celebrations include processions in traditional costumes, folk dance performances, and impressive feasts.

Guelaguetza means "offering" or "**reciprocal** exchange of gifts and services." Celebrations take place across Oaxaca region, especially in the city of Oaxaca.

Closer Look

Dia de los Muertos decorations are meant to show respect and love for deceased loved ones.

Dia de los Muertos

The *Dia de los Muertos,* or Day of the Dead, festival is rooted in ancient Aztec culture. The Aztecs believed that human souls exist forever. They rest in *Mictlan,* the mythical underworld of the Aztecs. But once a year, they were believed to travel to the world of the living to visit family and friends. This was a difficult journey, so family members provided food, water, and small items to help guide them.

These traditions live on in modern Mexico, which celebrates *Dia de los Muertos* every November 1 and 2. In towns across Mexico, people celebrate by dressing up in costumes, taking part in parades, and hosting parties with singing and dancing. Some families leave small offerings on the graves of their ancestors. Others erect small altars—or *ofrendas*—in their homes to welcome their visitors from the afterlife. Calaveras, ornately decorated representations of a skull, are incredibly popular on *Dia de los Muertos*. Rather than something to be feared, death in Mexico is celebrated as part of the cycle of life and an opportunity to honor family ancestors. In this way, ancient attitudes towards death have greatly shaped modern beliefs.

Ofrendas usually include photos of deceased family members, their favorite foods, and other items to make them feel at home, such as toys for deceased children. Statues and photos of saints and decorations such as candles and flowers are also included. Sometimes, families may also leave a washbasin for the deceased to refresh themselves after making the journey to the world of the living.

Food

While each region has its own style of Mexican cuisine, three items are grown throughout the country: corn, beans, and squash. Together, they form the basis of Mexican cuisine—from tamales and burritos to tortillas, tacos, and enchiladas. Locally grown avocados, chili peppers, tomatoes, and potatoes are often featured in stuffings or side dishes. In coastal areas where seafood is abundant, *pulpo* (octopus) and *ceviche* (seafood marinated in lime or lemon) are popular. Some foods have evolved from a combination of Spanish and Indigenous dishes. *Puchero*—a stew named for the clay pot in which it is cooked—was adapted by the Spanish to include local ingredients.

Mexico's national dance—the *Jarabe Tapatio*—has its roots in Spain. It celebrates the courtship of a man and a woman and features a man's sombrero.

Chilaquiles is a traditional Mexican breakfast dish made from leftover dinner tortilla and salsa. It can be topped with eggs, rice, chicken, avocado, and more.

Music and Dance

Music and dance are important elements in Mexico's festivals. Mariachi music, for which the country is famous, uses stringed instruments with Spanish origins. But its name likely came from an Indigenous language. Many folk dances are rooted in agricultural traditions and feature costumes made of local materials including animal hides, bird feathers, and shells. Sonora region's Danza del Venado features a deer—whose spirit is worshipped among Indigenous peoples—being pursued by a group of hunters. Dancers in the Acatlaxquis hold sugar cane stalks or reeds in a performance that asks for fertile land and abundant harvests.

Closer Look

This man wears the traditional clothing of the *charro*, or cowboy. It is an example of traditional clothing that celebrates Mexican history and is associated with the country by many around the world.

Charreada and Charros

The rodeo—or *charreada*—is Mexico's official national sport. It dates back to the 1600s, when the Spanish introduced horses to Mexico to help manage the large cattle ranches they had established. At first, the government made it illegal for Indigenous people to ride horses, unless it was necessary as part of their work for the Spanish landowners. They wanted to keep the power of horses for themselves. Indigenous people were also forbidden to dress in the same fashion as Spanish riders. So instead, they invented a new fashion, which featured tight fitting suits decorated with bright embroidery and a wide-brimmed sombrero. As these Mexican *charros* –or cowboys— perfected their riding talents, charreadas became a popular way for them to show off their roping, branding, and herding skills. The Day of the Charro is celebrated every year on September 14 with competitions and parades.

In addition to the Day of the Charro, Charro Days are held every year in February as a celebration of friendship between the people of Brownsville, Texas, and Matamoros, Tamaulipas, Mexico. This young boy takes part in the celebration in Matamoros.

CHAPTER 5

Looking to the Future

Protecting Indigenous Rights and Lands

Indigenous culture plays an important role in everyday life and influences Mexican food, culture, art, and traditions. It is bound together by customs and beliefs that are deeply rooted in nature and the environment. Trees, rivers, wind, rain, the Sun, the earth, and the sky are believed to have their own spirits. Each dictates the rhythms of life for Indigenous peoples.

From the era of Spanish colonization to the twenty-first century, Indigenous peoples have had to fight for their right to the land on which they live, work, and grow food. Illegal logging, along with expanded mining and ranching operations, have encroached upon many areas in which they have lived for centuries. Tens of thousands of Indígenas have been forcibly displaced from their lands.

This young girl takes part in a cultural festival in Atlixco, Puebla, Mexico. This is one way Indigenous traditions are passed to younger generations in Mexico.

Mining operations often leave the land uninhabitable and barren.

In 2020, Otomí people occupied the offices of the National Institute of Indigenous Peoples. They refused to leave until their demands for better living and working conditions during the COVID-19 pandemic were met. They faced increased risk due to overcrowded living areas and a lack of clean, running water. In response, the government agreed to meet with them to come to a solution.

Government Action

In 1996, the Mexican government signed the San Andres Peace Accords. This agreement recognized the rights of Indigenous peoples and aimed to increase their participation in government and important policy decisions. It was also designed to advance policies to promote the rights of Indigenous women and children. Critics argue that many of its commitments have not been met.

Mexico was one of 144 countries that adopted the UN Declaration on the Rights of Indigenous Peoples in 2007. But despite the policies created to support this declaration, many of Mexico's Indigenous communities continue to face discrimination and marginalization. More than 40 percent of Indigenous Mexicans live in extreme poverty.

Despite policies that promote Indigenous rights, Indigenous Mexicans continue to be poorly represented in government, business, and community. Some feel they must adopt more modern or mestizo ways in order to be successful in Mexico's economy. More government action needs to be done to ensure the survival of their culture and the well-being and success of their people.

Challenges of Climate Change

Mexico's geography and climate make it especially vulnerable to extreme weather events. Climate change has caused frequent droughts and difficult growing conditions for farmers. Large areas of farmland have been damaged or lost due to soil erosion and **degradation**. As conditions become more difficult to cultivate crops, farmers are leaving their land and migrating to cities in search of a secure livelihood for their families.

Corn crops have been the foundation of Mexican settlement for thousands of years. But as **water insecurity** has increased, farmers have turned to other crops that require less water—such as pistachio nuts and cacti—for their livelihoods. Water insecurity will pose long-term risks to food security for the Mexican people. In some farming regions, researchers and farmers are returning to agricultural strategies based on ancient farming techniques.

Scientists are studying strains of drought- and pest-resistant corn and beans. This could be a solution for farmers who depend on these crops.

pistachio tree

Deforestation intensifies soil erosion, since tree and plant roots are no longer there to hold soil in place.

These farmers are planting amaranth, an ancient grain native to Mexico. In the region of Oaxaca, there is a growing movement by Mexican farmers and chefs to revive native crops such as amaranth, which is also drought-resistant. It is a way to strengthen the local economy and also promote healthy food in local communities.

New Agricultural Strategies

The cafetal is a farming system rooted in ancient practices. It involves a multi-level system of agriculture including tall trees, mid-level plants like coffee, and ground-level vegetables and vines. The plants support and protect one another while using water, sunlight, and soil nutrients more efficiently. Intercropping is another traditional method of growing crops that work well together. Corn, beans, and squash are the best-known group of plants that have been grown together for centuries in Mexico. They seem uniquely suited to help one another resist pests, preserve nutrients, and maximize water efficiency.

A modern strategy involving agriculture and energy production uses modern technology to turn cacti waste into biofuel. The prickly pear cactus fruit is used in many Mexican foods, medicines, and cosmetics. The plant requires little water and can be harvested many times a year, making it a **profitable** crop. Large parts of the plants are thrown away as the fruit is harvested. But scientists have found a way to turn the cacti waste into biofuel, making it a more environmentally friendly crop.

Biofuel is fuel that comes from living things, such as plant materials or animal waste. It is a source of renewable energy.

New Rules for Urbanization

As cities have become Mexico's engines for growth and prosperity, there has been a shift away from the traditions of rural agricultural communities and their connection to the land. Cities generate 90 percent of Mexico's economic output. But an increase in **urbanization** also brings new challenges. Water insecurity, air pollution, and social inequality are real issues for many urban Mexicans.

Much of Mexico's urban growth has happened on the outer edges of cities, where **informal settlements** have sprung up. Many of these have little or no services, such as schools. Lack of proper roads and public transit means people face long and challenging commutes to work, school, and hospitals. This creates an environment of inequality for access to jobs, education, and health care. Strategies for development of cities are needed to ensure urban areas are sustainable and resilient. All levels of government—from local to state level—need to work together to enforce policies to manage growth while protecting the environment.

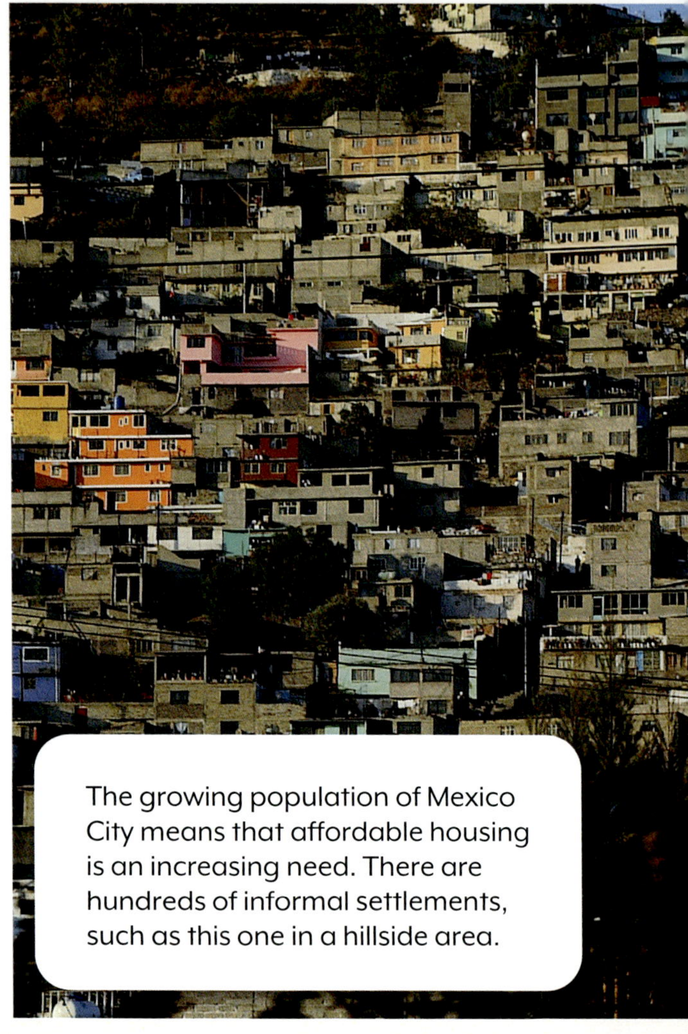

The growing population of Mexico City means that affordable housing is an increasing need. There are hundreds of informal settlements, such as this one in a hillside area.

As cities expand, traffic is a big issue and contributes to the problem of air pollution.

Street Vendors

Street vendors have long been an important part of Mexico's urban culture, providing employment and affordable food and services for more than 1 million people. Many people feel these vendors add to the vibrant nature of Mexico City's urban lifestyle. But others feel that these informal and somewhat unregulated services do not fit with Mexico City's modern urban cityscapes. Strong urban design and clear regulations could help ensure that activities such as these can continue to prosper and add to Mexico City's unique culture and diversity.

Many people in Mexico City depend on street vendors for easier access to affordable food and goods.

Some vendors sell their goods in public markets, such as this one near the center of Mexico City.

barren Land on which very few plants grow

carbon A chemical element that forms one of the bases of living things. Carbon compounds such as carbon dioxide contribute to climate change.

cochineal A red dye that is made from insects

cocoliztli A deadly illness that killed millions of people, especially Aztecs, in the 1500s in New Spain, or present-day Mexico

colonize The process by which a country takes control of another country or area by occupying it

commerce The activity of buying and selling goods and services

commercial Concerned with buying and selling goods and services

communal Shared by members of a community

conquistadors Spanish conquerors who set out to colonize what they called the "New World," or the Americas

craggy A rough or uneven cliff or rock surface

deforestation The practice of clearing wide areas of forest for other uses, such as farming

degradation Deteriorating or making something worse or weaker

deported Forced to leave a country

dialects Forms of languages that are specific to regions or groups

domesticated Crops that are adapted over time for human use

eco-tourism Tourism that involves environmentally friendly travel and that promotes conservation

encroached Intruded on

epidemic The rapid spread of a disease within a population at a certain time

excavations The processes of digging, uncovering, and processing archaeological remains

exploited Used something or someone unfairly for your own advantage

fertile Able to produce crops

free market An economic system in which goods are bought and sold with few or no government restrictions

Indigenous Native to a particular place. Indigenous people are the original inhabitants of a place.

indigo A dark blue dye that comes from the indigo plant

industrialization The process by which an area or country changes from mostly agricultural to more industry-based, focused on manufacturing goods

informal jobs Employment without an established agreement or contract, often with a lack of protection for workers

informal settlement Groups of houses, often crowded and makeshift, illegally constructed on public land. People living in informal settlements are often forced there due to a lack of affordable housing or after losing their homes in events such as natural disasters.

interplanting The practice of planting certain crops alongside each other to maximize land use and crop yield

irrigation The agricultural process of supplying water to crops

Latin America The countries in South and North America that were once Spanish or Portugese colonies, in which many people speak Spanish or Portugese

marginalized Treated as insignificant or unimportant

missionaries People sent to do religious work and spread their religion in another country

nomadic Moving from place to place

obsidian A dark, glasslike rock formed from cooling lava

plateau A flat area that is higher in altitude than the surrounding land

precarious Vulnerable or in danger

profitable Making profit, or money beyond expenses

reciprocal Given in return or equal actions

reserves Supplies of a natural resource that are available but not needed immediately

sparse Thinly scattered

subtropical Climate regions that are warm, with a high amount of rainfall, but that have cooler temperatures than tropical regions at the equator

sustainable Able to be used in a way that does not deplete natural resources or cause significant environmental damage

temperate Climate regions without extreme temperatures and with moderate rainfall

textile Cloth or woven fabric

urbanization The process by which an area or country changes from mostly rural to more urban, with more cities

water insecurity Not having a reliable and steady supply of clean water

World Heritage Site A protected landmark or area singled out by the United Nations Educational, Scientific, and Cultural Organization (UNESCO) as being globally significant

Books

DK Children. *Aztecs, Inca and Maya*. DK Children, 2011.

Maddicks, Russell. *Mexico – Culture Smart!: The Essential Guide to Customs and Culture*. Kuperard, 2017.

O'Neill, Bill. *The Great Book of Mexico*. LAK Publishing, 2020.

Sonneborn, Liz. *Mexico – Enchantment of the World*. Children's Press, 2017.

Websites

www.nationalgeographic.org/topics/resource-library-mesoamerica/?q=&page=1&per_page=25
Learn more about early civilizations that inhabited Mexico and Central America, with links to further reading.

https://kids.britannica.com/kids/article/Mexico/345743
An introduction to the people, geography, and history of Mexico.

https://instituteofmexicodc.org/index.php/mexico-for-you/
Explore the Mexican Cultural Insitute's free "Mexico for You" booklet, which has detailed information about Mexico's history, important figures, environment, and culture.

About the Author

Linda Barghoorn has written thirty children's books for which she studied a wide range of topics from deserts and earthquakes to refugees, resilient cities to remarkable people. She is an avid learner, explorer and traveler. When she's not at work, she can most often be found hiking or curled up with a good book.